2CELLOS

LUKA SULIC & STJEPAN HAUSER

Arranged by Dan Geisler
Edited by Peter Thomas

ISBN 978-1-4584-1801-2

7777 W. BLUEMOUND RD. P.O. BOX 13819 MILWAUKEE, WI 53213

Visit Hal Leonard Online at
www.halleonard.com

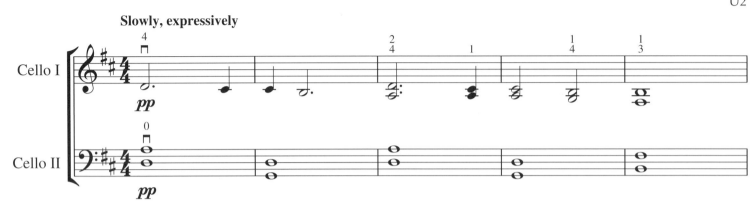

WHERE THE STREETS HAVE NO NAME

Words and Music by
U2

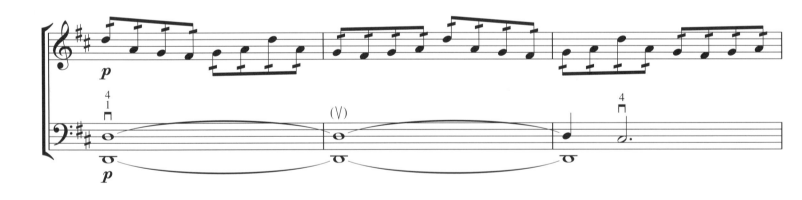

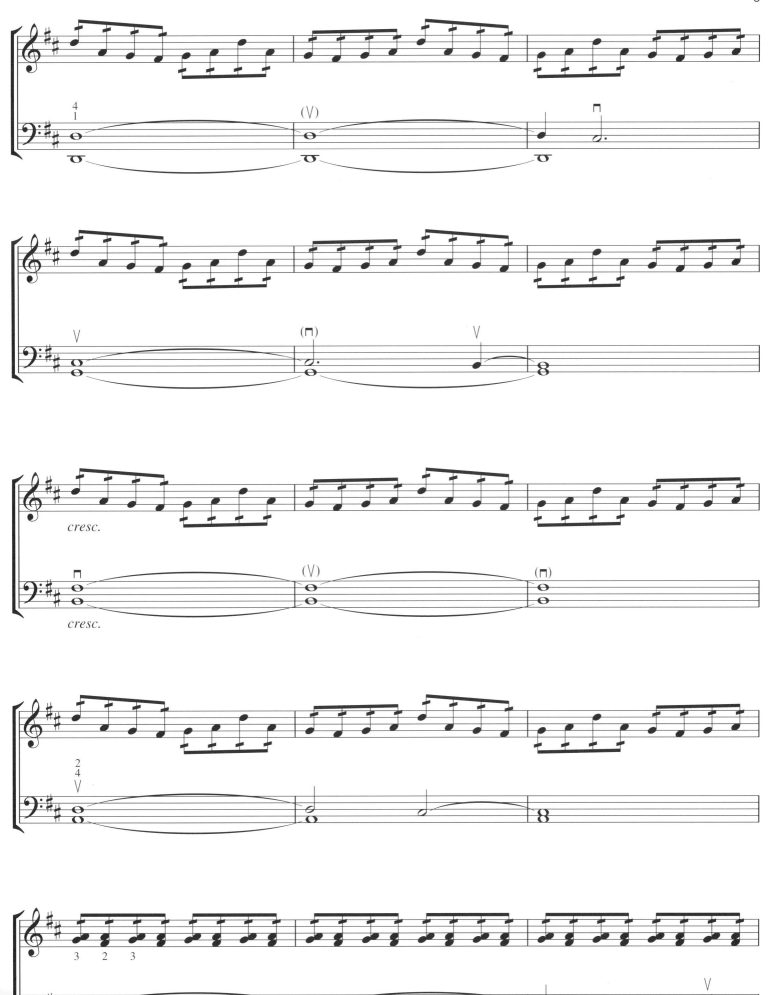

4

MISIRLOU

Words by FRED WISE,
MILTON LEEDS, JOSE PINA and SIDNEY RUSSELL
Music by NICOLAS ROUBANIS

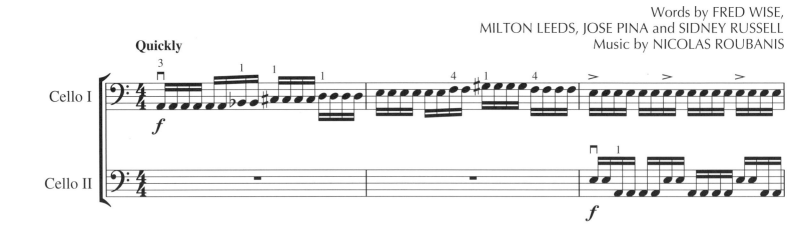

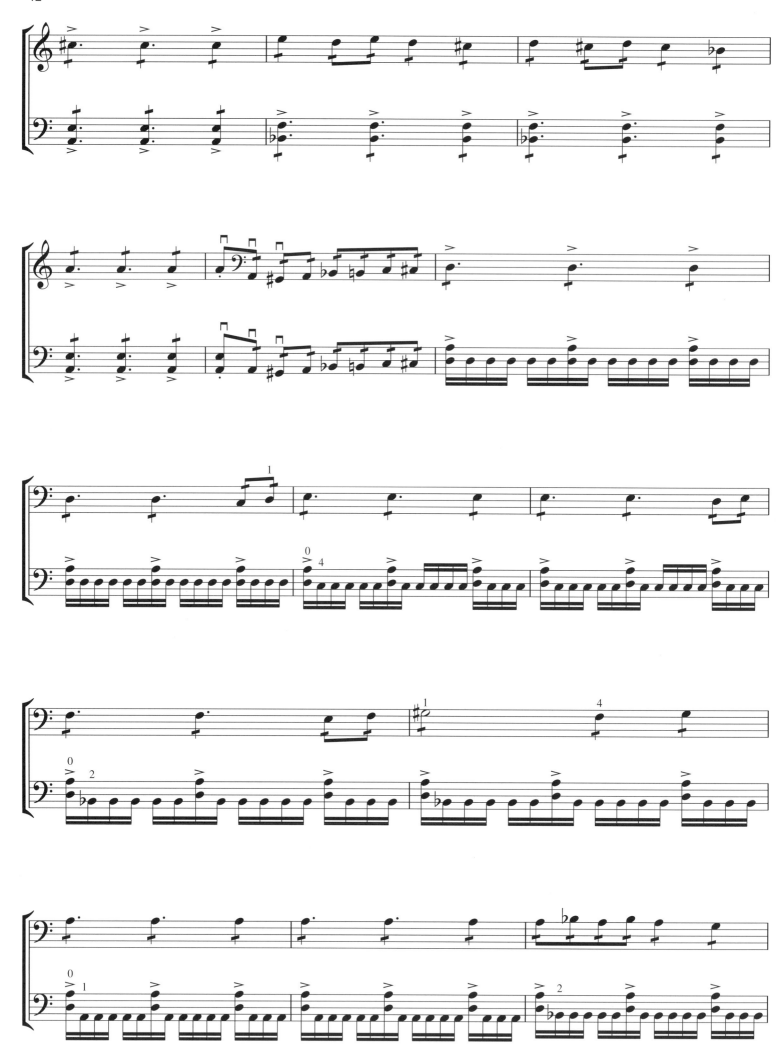

USE SOMEBODY

Words and Music by CALEB FOLLOWILL,
NATHAN FOLLOWILL, JARED FOLLOWILL
and MATTHEW FOLLOWILL

SMOOTH CRIMINAL

Words and Music by
MICHAEL JACKSON

32

FRAGILE

Music and Lyrics by
STING

*Use hand to strike body of cello.

40

RESISTANCE

Words and Music by
MATTHEW BELLAMY

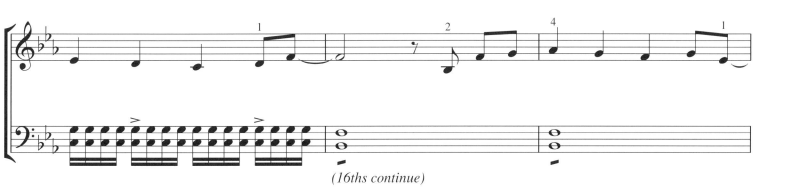

(16ths continue)

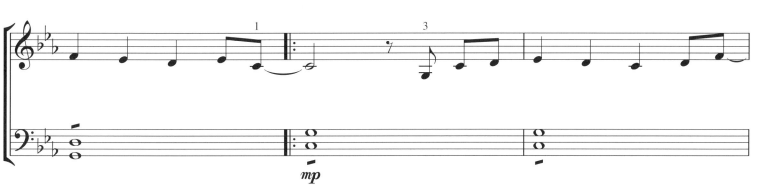

cresc. to end

cresc. to end

ff

ff

WELCOME TO THE JUNGLE

Words and Music by W. AXL ROSE,
SLASH, IZZY STRADLIN',
DUFF McKAGAN and STEVEN ADLER

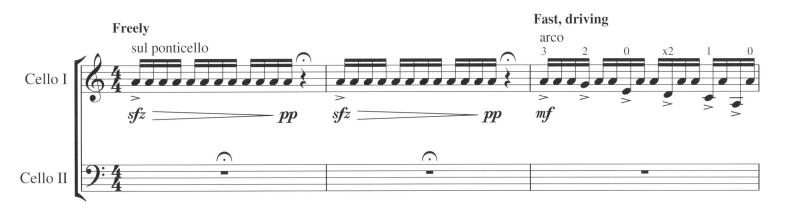

48

(16ths continue)

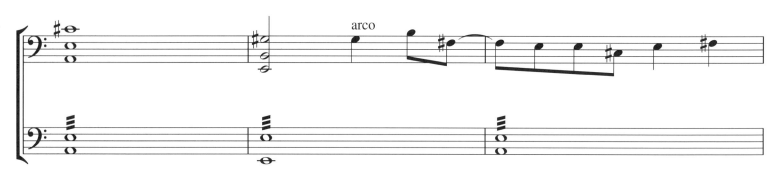

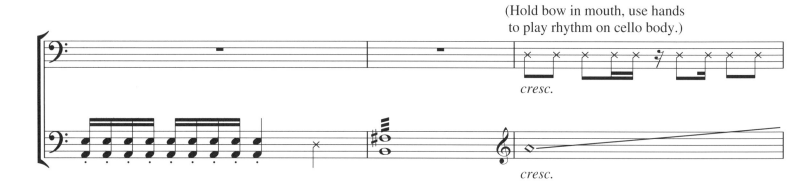

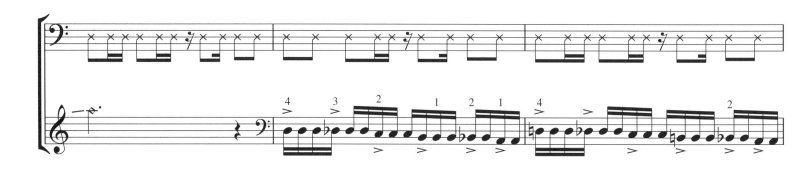

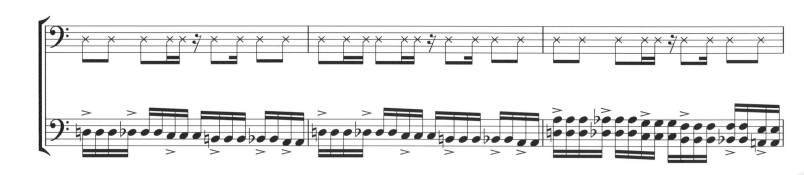

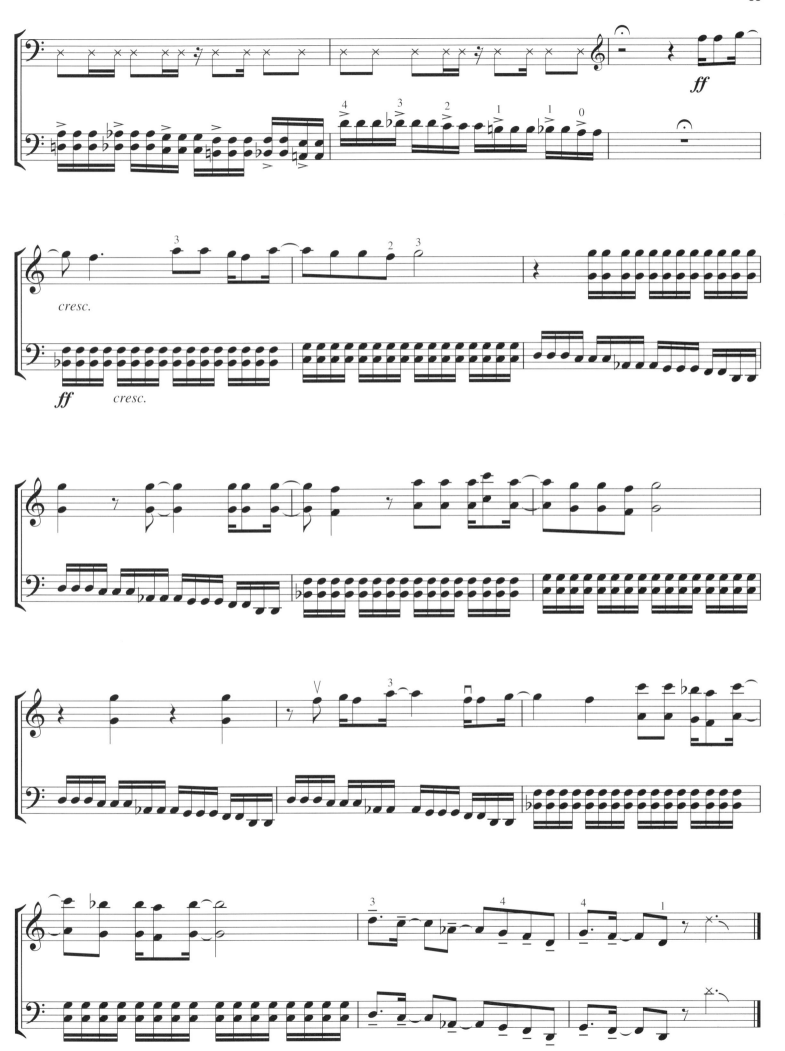

HUMAN NATURE

Words and Music by JOHN BETTIS
and STEVE PORCARO

*Percussive hand strike on body of cello.

58

Repeat and Fade

Optional Ending

VIVA LA VIDA

Words and Music by GUY BERRYMAN,
JON BUCKLAND, WILL CHAMPION
and CHRIS MARTIN

60

sub. **pp**

sub. **pp**

1.–3.

4.

SMELLS LIKE TEEN SPIRIT

Words and Music by KURT COBAIN,
KRIST NOVOSELIC and DAVE GROHL

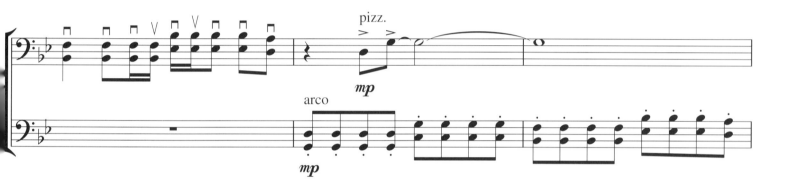

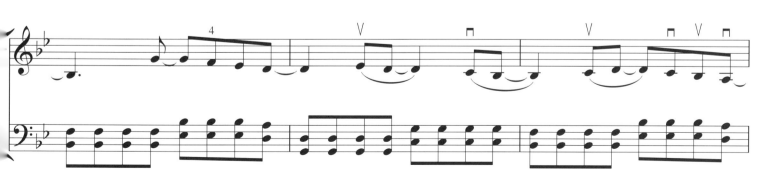

Play 3 times

WITH OR WITHOUT YOU

Words and Music by
U2

Moderately, expressively

Cello I

Cello II

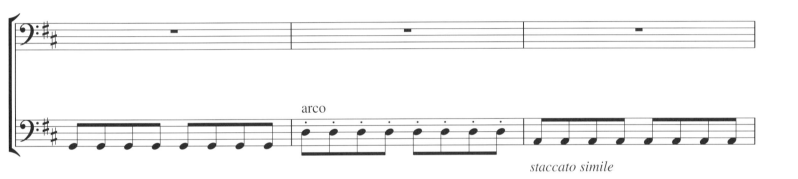

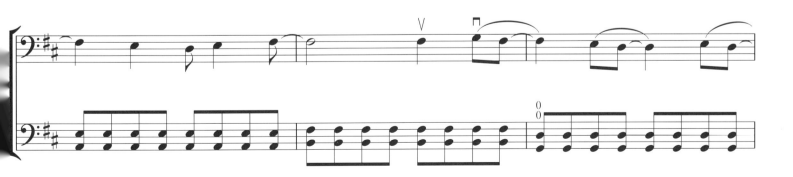